Café Daughter

Café Daughter

Kenneth T. Williams

Café Daughter
first published 2013 by
Scirocco Drama
An imprint of J. Gordon Shillingford Publishing Inc.
© 2013 Kenneth T. Williams

Scirocco Drama Editor: Glenda MacFarlane
Cover design by Terry Gallagher/Doowah Design Inc.
Author photo by Stefen Winchester
Printed and bound in Canada on 100% post-consumer recycled paper.

We acknowledge the financial support of the Manitoba Arts Council and The Canada
Council for the Arts for our publishing program.

Library and Archives Canada Cataloguing in Publication

Williams, Kenneth T., 1965-
    Café Daughter/Kenneth T. Williams

A play.
ISBN 978-1-897289-85-3

    I. Title.

PS8645.I4525C33 2013   C812'.6   C2012-908516-2

J. Gordon Shillingford Publishing
P.O. Box 86, RPO Corydon Avenue, Winnipeg, MB Canada R3M 3S3

*Dedicated to the memories of Quan Leen Yok (Happy)
and Eva McNab Quan.*

Acknowledgements

Writing *Café Daughter* would not have been possible without the financial assistance of the Canada Council for the Arts and the Ontario Arts Council Chalmers Award. I would also like to thank the Banff Playwrights Colony, Gwaandak Theatre Society, Persephone Theatre, Maureen LaBonte, Rachel Ditor, Johnna Wright, Elinor Holt, Jamie Lee Shebelski, Carol Greyeyes, Yvette Nolan, PJ Prudat and Keith Lock. It's impossible to say how much I owe to the generosity of Sen. Dr. Lillian Eva Quan Dyck, Winston Quan, the extended McNab Family, and the George Gordon First Nation for sharing their stories.

Production History

The Gwaandak Theatre Society produced the world premiere of *Café Daughter* in May 2011 in Dawson City, Yukon Territory, with the following cast:

YVETTE .... PJ Prudat

Directed by Yvette Nolan

Set Design by Linda Leon

Lighting Designer / Technical Director: Brendan Wiklund

Costume Design by Linda Talbot

Sound Design by Jona Barr

Stage Manager: Anne Taylor

Production Manager: Susie Anne Bartsch

Production Assistant / Stage Manager Apprentice: Emily Farrell

Setting

Act I - in the small farming town of Allistair, Saskatchewan.

Act II - in the small city of Saskatoon, Saskatchewan.

Time

Act I - Fall, 1957

Act II - Spring, 1964

Cast

All of the characters are played by one actress.

Yvette Wong: We see her as an adult, at 9 years old and 16 years old.

Katherine Wong: Yvette's mother, a beautiful Cree woman in her early 30s.

Charlie Wong: Yvette's father, a Chinese man who immigrated to Canada in the 1930s. In Act I he's in his late 50s, in Act II he's in his late 60s.

Doris: Yvette's aunt, early 20s in Act I, late 20s in Act II.

Amos: Yvette's Mushom, Katherine's father, mid 60s.

Dr. Thompson: Town doctor for Allistair.

Mr. Adams: Principal of the school in Allistair.

Miss Scott: Yvette's teacher in Allistair.

Richard: Yvette's classmate in Allistair.

Older Boy: A young thug.

Mr. Tanner: Yvette's math and physics teacher in Saskatoon, early 30s.

Maggie Wolf: A Mi'kmaq/English girl who attends Yvette's school in Saskatoon, 18, very pretty and cosmopolitan.

Kenneth T. Williams

Kenneth T. Williams is a Cree playwright, photographer and journalist from the George Gordon First Nation. His plays *Café Daughter, Gordon Winter, Thunderstick, Bannock Republic, Suicide Notes* and *Three Little Birds* have been professionally produced across Canada. *Thunderstick* has recently been optioned as a feature film project. *Thunderstick, Gordon Winter,* and *Bannock Republic* were published by Scirocco Drama, with *Suicide Notes* published in the anthology, *Three On the Boards,* by Signature Editions. He also teaches playwriting at the University of Saskatchewan. He is the first Aboriginal writer to earn an M.F.A. in playwriting from the University of Alberta. He currently resides in Saskatoon.

Act I

Scene 1

We see YVETTE as an adult. She's dressed in the university graduation gown of a medical doctor. She holds a diploma.

YVETTE: What am I afraid of?

She takes off her gowns and looks over the stage, we now see the café "Open/Closed sign," a table, a school desk, and a bed. She touches these things as if patching together the images from her past.

Doctors are supposed to know everything.

She sits on the bed.

This is when I knew I wanted to be a doctor.

She becomes nine-year-old YVETTE. It's now 1957, and we're in Allistair, Saskatchewan, in the family's café.

Shhhhhhhhhh. I have a secret. My mommy's very sick. The doctor is seeing her now. I can hear them talking. Whispering.

She listens intently.

He says something about a fever. And rashes... He says she has to go to Regina for some tests because he's not sure.

"We don't need to spend any money on doctors or hospitals or tests," says my mama. "I'll go see my dad. He'll have something for this." We're going to the reserve, Mama?

KATHERINE: Yes, my girl. Just pack a few things. And bring a book. It's a long drive.

YVETTE: Dad loads the car quickly. He's humming. And smiling. "It'll be good to see Amos again," he says. We all get in the car.

In the car.

KATHERINE: What book did you bring, baby?

YVETTE shows a book about pharoahs.

YVETTE: It's about ancient Egypt. Would you like to go to Egypt one day?

KATHERINE: *(Laughing.)* We can barely afford to go to Regina. That's why we have books. We can see them there when we can't see them in person.

YVETTE: I want to see the pyramids.

KATHERINE: Maybe one day, my girl. Maybe.

YVETTE reads a little.

YVETTE: I almost finish my book by the time we get to the reserve. I see little cabins here and there. I see a large building with a cross on it. Some children are outside. We pass by it slowly.

My dad asks my mom, "Isn't the turn off here? Near the school?" She doesn't answer. I know when my mama is mad. She gets all quiet and crosses her arms and just stares. *(She mimics this.)* I think she's mad because Dad's lost. "Isn't this where the house is supposed to be?" he asks again. He drives down a muddy road. My mom nods.

There's no house here. It's just a smoking pit. A woman who looks a lot like mama is picking through the ash. Mama gets out quickly and starts speaking to her. In Cree. Really fast. Really loud. *(To CHARLIE.)* What are they saying, Daddy? He says,

"Don't get out of the car."

YVETTE: Why not?

CHARLIE: Just don't.

YVETTE: Mama stops arguing with the other woman and they both walk towards the car. The other woman gets into the back and gives me a big hug.

DORIS: Look at you, little girl. You're growing up so fast. And you're growing up so pretty. *(Pause.)* Don't you remember me?

YVETTE shakes her head.

(Laughing.) I'm your Auntie Doris.

YVETTE: Auntie who? She keeps hugging me. I wish she wouldn't. She gives us directions and we see a clearing, just off the road, with a large canvas tent and a big iron stove next to it. There's an old woman by the stove. My Auntie Doris hauls me out of the car and she speaks Cree to the old woman. They both smile and laugh. Auntie Doris pushes me towards the old woman.

DORIS: Go and hug your Kokum Mary.

YVETTE: She hugs me really, really tight. I can't breathe. She's in a good mood. But my mama isn't. She gets out of the car they start arguing in Cree. All three of them. Auntie Doris starts to cry and says, "Dad will be back soon. He'll explain everything." *(Pause.)* It's very quiet. Everyone seems angry. Dad breaks the silence.

CHARLIE: Is that stove hot? I hope everyone likes pancakes.

YVETTE: He doesn't wait for an answer. He just grabs the groceries that were in the back of the car and carries them to the tent. Kokum Mary is cutting something on a stump. *(She looks.)* Eeeewwww. What are those?

DORIS:	Those? Those are muskrats. We're having them for supper.
YVETTE:	Really? Muskrat?
DORIS:	You mean you've never had muskrat before?
YVETTE:	I shake my head. Auntie Doris laughs. "What kind of Indian are you?" she asks.

"We've never had to eat muskrat," says my mama.

What's it taste like, mama? "You don't have to eat it if you don't want to," she says. A horse-drawn wagon rolls into the camp. It's full of men and lumber. The man driving the wagon jumps off and runs to me. I hide behind my mama.

"Don't you remember your mushom?" he asks.

"Dad, she hasn't seen you in a long time."

"Yes, well, whose fault is that?"

My mom bites her bottom lip.

"Give your mushom a hug."

Mama nudges me towards him and he grabs me in his strong arms and squeezes me.

AMOS:	My, you've gotten so big. *(To CHARLIE.)* Hey, Charlie, good to see you, young fella!
YVETTE:	He slaps my dad on the back and shakes his hand like this.

She mimes the handshake from CHARLIE's point of view—like he's shaking hands with an overly friendly giant.

He goes to my mom. "So my girl…" He stops. He looks worried and asks her something in Cree.

"Don't know. No energy. Lots of pain. Rashes. Hard to walk sometimes."

AMOS: I'll fix you up something for the pain right quick. How long you around?

KATHERINE: Maybe the weekend.

AMOS: Good to hear! You'll be good as new when I'm done with you. And you can help us build a new cabin.

KATHERINE: Dad! What happened to the old house? Did the principal really burn it down?

YVETTE: The principal burned down their house!

AMOS: I was teaching the boys some of the old songs. They were gettin' pretty good too. But the principal felt it was interfering with their "education." He didn't want them remembering any of their Indian ways.

Pause.

KATHERINE: So…there was no drinking?

Pause.

AMOS: Charlie, my friend, how's the café?

CHARLIE: We're doing OK, Amos. We're doing OK.

AMOS: Good. Good to hear.

YVETTE: Amos finds a jar then leaves the camp. I don't know why but I follow him…from a distance.

AMOS: Oh! You scared me. How long have you been there, my girl?

YVETTE: What are you doing?

AMOS: I'm making a tea for your mother.

YVETTE: Are you a doctor?

AMOS: Some people call me that.

YVETTE: Can you really make her better?

AMOS: If she wants me to but I have to find out what's wrong with her first. Come, little one. I have everything I need. Let's go back home for supper.

YVETTE: He takes my hand and we walk back to the camp. I see the muskrats lying in the roasting pan. Face up. *(She mimics the muskrats.)* I'm not very hungry. My auntie Doris sees me staring at the muskrats and laughs. She tears off a little piece and offers it to me.

DORIS: Come on, my girl. It's delicious.

YVETTE: Everyone is staring at me. I look at my mama. She just nods her head. So I take a bite. *(She bites, chews, makes a face, forces herself to finish it.)* Good thing Dad also made a bunch of pancakes. I eat those.

AMOS: Those were some mighty fine pancakes you cooked up there, Charlie. You're gonna make yourself a wonderful wife someday. Come over here, sir, and sit with me. You're not in your café here.

YVETTE: My dad is happy to sit with him and they roll up some cigarettes.

"Holy, my girl, are you ever a good dishwasher," says my Auntie Doris. "Are you like this at home?"

"I keep telling her it's more important to study than wash dishes." says Mama.

"What do you want to be when you grow up?" asks Auntie Doris.

A doctor.

My auntie and kokum laugh.

"A doctor! Who's putting those ideas in her head?" they ask.

"She can be a doctor if she wants," says Mama.

Just then we hear some cars beeping and some headlights scan the camp. Many men come up to shake my mushom's hand, offer condolences about the house and curse the principal of the residential school. Amos is the centre of attention. The men want to know what he plans to do about the house. Some say he should run for chief. They're getting angrier and angrier... And then a bottle starts getting passed around. My Mom's not happy. My dad doesn't notice. He's handed the bottle and he takes a swig. The laughter gets louder, the curses angrier.

KATHERINE: Yvette, baby. Get your father and get in the car.

YVETTE: Those other men frighten me.

KATHERINE: Now!

YVETTE: I take my papa's hand. *(To CHARLIE.)* Papa, we have to go to the car. He looks towards my mom and sees her standing. The look on her face scares me. Dad takes me to the car.

AMOS: Hey, Charlie, you're not leaving yet are you, my friend?

CHARLIE: Sorry Amos. Time for us to go.

AMOS: No. It's not time yet. You just got here.

CHARLIE: Take care, Amos.

YVETTE: Mushom Amos looks at my mama, as she hobbles towards us.

AMOS: What is it, my daughter?

KATHERINE: I need your help! That's why I came here! But you couldn't resist all this bullshit these men were feeding you or the whiskey when they offered it!

You can't make the medicine when you're drunk. You taught me that. But when your own daughter needs your healing you still couldn't resist a drink! And you'll be drunk for at least a week! Or a month! And I'm sure you were teaching those boys songs alright. Drinking songs!

AMOS: I'm sorry, my girl. Come back...later...and I'll doctor you.

KATHERINE: I'm never coming back.

AMOS: What? Don't say that.

KATHERINE: And neither is Yvette. She's never setting foot on this reserve again. And I don't want you coming around us. Ever. You hear me? Never. She's going to make something of herself. Maybe a doctor if she wants to be. But she doesn't need you drunken fools bringing her down. Stay away from us. You hear me? Stay away.

YVETTE: Dad starts the car and drives away. I can see Amos, the fire burning behind him. He's watching us. His shoulders heave up and down. He raises his hand, waving to me. I wave back.

KATHERINE: Turn around, baby. Turn around and never look at them again.

YVETTE: Why, mama?

KATHERINE: You're not one of them. Understand me? You're not an Indian. You never, ever tell anyone that you are.

YVETTE: Shhhhhhh. I have a secret. I'm an Indian... I promise not to tell anyone...ever.

Pause.

Scene 2

A school bell rings.

YVETTE: I'm never late for school. I'm always early. I try get there before the other kids. The playground is almost empty. An older boy, Richard, squints his eyes at me and smiles as if I have buck teeth and bow. *(She mimics this.)* "Aaaaaah soooo."

I don't have buck teeth.

She sits at her desk and opens a book about ancient Egypt.

The other kids are stuck in Allistair, Saskatchewan. I'm a priest of Anubis, preparing the pharaoh's body for mummification.

She reads and becomes aware of someone watching her.

Mr. Adams is by the door. He's the new principal. He just started this year.

MR. ADAMS: Yvette, why aren't you playing outside?

YVETTE: I prefer reading.

I show him my book.

MR. ADAMS: You understand this?

YVETTE: I'm on the mummification part. It's funny how the ancient Egyptians saved all the organs in pots for the pharaoh's soul but threw away the brain and then they filled the skull with straw and cotton. A lot of good that'll do him in the afterlife. A head full of straw.

MR. ADAMS: Indeed. Isn't this the slow learners class?

YVETTE: It is for the rest of them.

MR. ADAMS: What grade are you in?

YVETTE: Five.

MR. ADAMS: How old are you?

YVETTE: Nine. I'll be ten in a couple of weeks.

MR. ADAMS: When you go home for dinner, ask your parents if they can meet with me after school. Will you do that for me?

YVETTE: Am I in trouble?

MR. ADAMS: No, not at all. I just want to meet with them.

YVETTE: I don't care if he says I'm not in any trouble, a meeting with the principal is never good. *(Pause.)* It's after school. We're all in the principal's office. Mama, Dad, and me. They keep looking at me, as if I'm going to crack and finally admit that I'm in really big trouble. I'm not relieved when Mr. Adams comes into the office.

MR. ADAMS: Thank you for waiting, Mr. and Mrs. Wong.

YVETTE: Mama doesn't let him sit down. "What is this about?"

MR. ADAMS: *(Laughs.)* I can assure you, Yvette is not in any trouble, Mrs. Wong. I'm new here and I'm just getting to know the students and their families. I'm sorry it's taken so long to get to meet you but…I have to admit, I'm a little puzzled as to why Yvette's in the slow learners class. I've gone through her file and looked at all her grades, and they're the best in the school. Year after year. And I was hoping an answer would pop out at me but one didn't. She's definitely not slow. She doesn't belong there.

KATHERINE: We didn't put her there. The previous principal did.

YVETTE: "I see," he says. "That doesn't make any sense at all." Just then, Miss Scott walks in. She's super surprised to see us.

MISS SCOTT: I'm sorry, you're busy. I was told you wanted to see me.

MR. ADAMS: Come in, Miss Scott. You know the Wongs, correct?

MISS SCOTT: Uh, no, we actually haven't met…properly.

MR. ADAMS: Mr. and Mrs. Wong, Miss Scott is our grade six and seven teacher. I'm moving Yvette into your class Miss Scott.

MISS SCOTT: Excuse me! My class? But she's…she's…

MR. ADAMS: Supposed to be in grade five?

MISS SCOTT: No. Well, yes, that, but…she's… You have to understand Mr. Adams… The other parents… well…the other parents might object to having Yvette in the same class as their children. That's why she was better suited in the slow class.

MR. ADAMS: Because those parents were less likely to complain that a Chinese girl was in there.

MISS SCOTT: *(Relieved.)* Exactly! You understand completely. Is there anything else?

MR. ADAMS: Yes, there is. Yvette, do you still have that book on Egypt with you?

YVETTE: I hand him my book. He shows it to Miss Scott.

MR. ADAMS: Miss Scott, can you tell me if any of your grade six students have read a book like this?

MISS SCOTT: You have to understand these children, Mr. Adams. It's hard enough to get them to read a book when it's on the curriculum. If they don't have to read it, they're not going to read it.

MR. ADAMS: I know. Yvette read this on her own. And she described it to me. It showed a superior understanding of the material. Very difficult material I may add. She's way too advanced for grade five.

MISS SCOTT: Well, that's fine, Mr. Adams. But do you have to move her into my class?

MR. ADAMS: You have to understand, Miss Scott. You're the only grade six teacher we have. That's if it's OK with Mr. and Mrs. Wong.

YVETTE: My parents look at me.

"Yvette, what do you think, honey?"

What do I think? What am I supposed to think? I'm just a kid.

MISS SCOTT: You know, Mr. and Mrs. Wong, Yvette has obviously been thriving in her class till now.

MR. ADAMS: Miss Scott, please. *(To YVETTE.)* Yvette?

YVETTE: I say it before I know what I'm saying. *(To MR. ADAMS.)* Yes, I'd like to go into grade six.

MR. ADAMS: Then it's settled. Welcome to grade six, Yvette. Mr. and Mrs. Wong, you should be very proud.

YVETTE: We are, says Mama.

Scene 3

YVETTE: The next day, I arrive early for class…it's the normal time for me but Miss Scott is surprised to see me.

"Pick an empty desk," she says.

All the desks have names on them except the one in the back with a square drawn around it.

Is this where you put the dumb kids?

MISS SCOTT sighs.

MISS SCOTT: Only when I have to. It will have to do for now. Make yourself a name card while I prepare for today's lessons.

YVETTE: If they think I'm the dumb kid, they have another think coming.

She prints out her name on cardboard and places it on her desk.

Some other children come in and see me in "the dumb kid desk." I'm not supposed to be in their class. They freeze, look at each other wondering if they've got the right room, then to Miss Scott. They whisper to each other.

Miss Scott doesn't even look up and says, "Be quiet and sit down, children."

They obey…somewhat…more whispers. I can hear some of it. Then Richard walks in.

"What the heck is the Chinaman doing here?" he whispers. "She's in the dummy desk!"

MISS SCOTT: *(Raps the desk with a ruler.)* I said, quiet.

YVETTE: Silence. Miss Scott runs a tight ship.

MISS SCOTT: You've all noticed that we have a new student with us. She's no stranger to the school. Yvette, would you please come to the front and introduce yourself…properly.

YVETTE: Aaaaah geeze. I hate doing this. Miss Scott looks at me and snaps her fingers.

"Chop chop, Miss Wong," she says.

I march to the front of the class.

My name's Yvette Wong. I'm going to be ten years old soon. I'm now in grade six. My parents own the café in town here. I like reading. And I want to be a doctor when I grow up.

MISS SCOTT: Maybe Yvette meant she wants to be a nurse. Women can be nurses. They don't become doctors.

YVETTE: But I want to be a doctor, Miss Scott. I want to heal people who are sick.

MISS SCOTT: That is all, Yvette. Thank you. You may sit down now. Alright, class. We have the fall pageant next month. And I thought we could do a play. It's called, *Laura Secord, the Heroine of 1812*.

YVETTE: A play! This is wonderful news.

"What kind of play Miss Scott?"

"Can we sing Miss Scott?"

"I want to be a cowboy Miss Scott."

She calls for quiet and there's a nervous silence. She then starts calling out who will be playing what.

MISS SCOTT: And Yvette...Yvette!

YVETTE: Miss Scott?

MISS SCOTT: You're going to be the Indian Chief.

YVETTE: Indian...Chief? But I'm not...Indian.

MISS SCOTT: It's just a play. You can pretend to be an Indian. You're the only one here who looks anything like the part. If someone didn't know it, they'd think you were some kind of Indian.

    Pause.

YVETTE: Thank you, Miss Scott.

I'd never been asked to be in a play before. So after school, I run home. I can't wait to tell them the good news. Mama! Papa!

Pause.

Something's wrong. It's really quiet. It's never this quiet.

(Cautiously.) Mama? Papa? *(No answer. Louder.)* Mama?

Pause.

Papa?

KATHERINE: Happy birthday, my girl!

YVETTE jumps and shrieks.

YVETTE: A bike! They're holding a bike!

She dances around excitedly. She gives big hugs to her mom and dad.

But my birthday isn't till next week.

CHARLIE: It arrived early. There was no way we could hide this for a week.

YVETTE: Can I ride it? I want to ride it. Pleeeeeeeeze.

CHARLIE: Cake first, then bicycle.

She blows out the candles.

YVETTE: Can we go now? Please, can we, please?

CHARLIE: OK, OK. Let's go, let's go.

CHARLIE holds the seat, pushing it around the stage. YVETTE is uneasy.

Easy, easy. Try and get some speed up. Are you ready? I'm going to let go now. Ready?

YVETTE, on the bike, unsteady but determined.

YVETTE: Ready!

              YVETTE struggles with the bike and wobbles here and there. Then she falls off.

              Ow!

              She rubs her knee.

CHARLIE: Maybe we should rest for a bit.

YVETTE: *(Pleading.)* Just a little longer?

CHARLIE: Cake now.

YVETTE: OK.

              My mama has cut the cake and served it on little plates.

KATHERINE: So what did you do in school today?

YVETTE: Oh! I'm going to be an Indian chief!

              Mama coughs and nearly chokes on her cake.

              (Coughing.) "Pardon me?" she asks.

              It's for the fall pageant. The class is doing a play. And I'm in it. I'm playing the Mohawk chief who helped the British in the War of 1812. It's about Laura Secord.

CHARLIE: Who's Laura Secord?

KATHERINE: *(Rising bitterness.)* She warned the British about an American sneak attack. Mohawk warriors escorted her. The principal at the school used them as an example of what "good Indians" could do. *(She snaps out of it.)* But I'm happy for you baby. You get to be in the school play. I never got to be in a play before.

YVETTE: Can I ride my bike to school tomorrow?

KATHERINE: OK.

Scene 4

Fifties rock plays in the background.

YVETTE: It's Saturday. I'm memorizing my lines. Some older boys are playing the new jukebox. My dad hates rock and roll but this is the only jukebox in town and it brings in a lot of customers.

The music suddenly stops.

OLDER BOY: Hey Chinaman! Your machine's busted. It took my nickel!

CHARLIE: The song ended.

OLDER BOY: It took my nickel!

CHARLIE: *(Getting angry.)* I just heard the song end. That was your song, right?

OLDER BOY: You calling me a liar, Chink!

CHARLIE: *(Livid.)* Get out! Get out before I call your father!

YVETTE: I've never seen my father so mad. The boys leave. Slowly. Whispering, "Dirty Chink thief."

CHARLIE: And don't come back!

Pause.

YVETTE: Dad? Am I a Chink?

Pause.

Scene 5

YVETTE: Miss Scott is teaching me to be an Indian.

(*Trying to remember her lines.*) White chief say true: we good King George's men. My warriors yell! Hide! Shoot! Hot bullet fly, like dart of Annee-meekee. We keep damn Long-Knife back. I just go now.

She grunts.

MISS SCOTT: What was that, Yvette? Was that supposed to be a grunt of satisfaction? The script says the Indian grunts with satisfaction. Do it again.

YVETTE grunts again.

No, no, no. Do it again.

YVETTE grunts, trying to sound more satisfied.

Look. Let's work on your other lines. Speak more haltingly, more like an Indian. Do you know what I mean?

YVETTE: I think so.

MISS SCOTT: Then do it again.

YVETTE: White chief say true: We good King—

MISS SCOTT: (*Interrupts.*) Like this. (*She then proceeds to act in the most horrifyingly, stereotypical way.*) "My warriors yell! Hide! Shoot! Hot bullet fly like dart of Annee-meekee." You see, just like that. Now you do it.

YVETTE copies MISS SCOTT action for action.

YVETTE: My warriors yell! Hide! Shoot! Hot bullet fly like dart of Annee-meekee.

MISS SCOTT: Perfect! We'll make an Indian out of you yet.

YVETTE: I run home.

Mama, Papa! I'm a real Indian! Miss Scott says so. She says I'm the best Indian she's ever seen.

CHARLIE: *(Laughs.)* You should tell your mother.

YVETTE: I run up the stairs. I see her lying in bed. Still.

Mama?

She doesn't move or look at me. I touch her arm.

Mama. You're hot. Really hot!

I run downstairs and grab Dad.

(To CHARLIE.) Mama's really hot. We need ice.

He runs to Mama's side. He touches her arm and forehead. Gently.

CHARLIE: Go get Dr. Thompson.

YVETTE: I run like the devil to Dr. Thompson's house. I pound on the door. He answers. Before I can say anything he shouts over his shoulder.

DR. THOMPSON: Dear! I have to go to the Wongs!

YVETTE: When we get back home, he tries to make me leave the room.

No! I want to stay with Mama!

(Whispering, laboured.) "My girl, wait with Daddy downstairs."

When I get downstairs, it's like the half the town is here. There's Reverend Smith and his wife. She reaches for me as if to hug me. It scares me. Reverend Smith tells Dad he's praying for Mama. My dad thanks them and says everything is fine.

(To CHARLIE.) Why are they praying for Mama?

CHARLIE: They're being nice.

YVETTE: Dad makes tea for everyone. It's quiet. The adults won't look at me. Dr. Thompson comes downstairs.

                  (To DR. THOMPSON.) Is my mama going die?

DR. THOMPSON: No, no, my dear. She has a very serious fever. I've given her some penicillin.

YVETTE: Will she get better?

DR. THOMPSON: We'll know in the next few hours. Watch her fever. If it suddenly goes up, let me know right away. Otherwise, I'll be back to give her another injection in a few hours.

YVETTE: I run upstairs to my mom. She's lying on the bed, breathing slowly.

                  (To KATHERINE.) I'm here, Mama. I'm not going anywhere.

KATHERINE: *(Weakly.)* Thank you baby. But I feel a lot better. I don't think this is necessary. The penicillin seems to be working. I really really want to get out of bed.

YVETTE: No. You stay in bed. You're not better. You're just acting like it. I'm not dumb. I know penicillin doesn't work that fast. You're sick and you need rest.

                  Pause.

KATHERINE: Then make me a cup of tea.

YVETTE: The next day, I ride my bike to school and park it in the racks. Why is everyone is looking at me? They're whispering and pointing. I walk into the class and sit down. Richard is standing with a group of boys. He slowly walks towards me. Uh-oh, this can't be good.

RICHARD: Sorry to hear about your mom. Hey, is it true that Chinese women turn into snakes when they die? That would be something to see. So did she?

YVETTE: She didn't die.

RICHARD: Really? It's all over town that your mother died last night. And then turned into a snake, I guess.

YVETTE: She's not Chinese.

RICHARD: Then what is she?

Pause.

YVETTE: Irish.

RICHARD: She doesn't look Irish.

YVETTE: Her last name was O'Neil.

RICHARD: Isn't that illegal or something? Chinese men marrying white women.

YVETTE: I don't know. Why don't you ask a policeman?

Miss Scott walks in and is about to take her seat when she sees me.

MISS SCOTT: *(Whispering.)* How are you doing, Yvette?

YVETTE: I'm fine. My mother's fine. She didn't die. She's just sick.

MISS SCOTT: Oh. I see. I can still excuse you if you don't feel like being here.

YVETTE: She told me to come to school, Miss Scott, so I won't keep telling her to stay in bed. Like the doctor told her.

MISS SCOTT: Oh. Well. Alright then. Take your seat.

RICHARD: Miss Scott, do Chinese women turn into snakes when they die?

MISS SCOTT: Pardon me, Richard?

RICHARD: Do Chinese women—

MISS SCOTT: *(Cutting him off.)* I heard your question. I just can't believe that you'd be so insensitive to Yvette. Apologize right now!

RICHARD: But her mother's not Chinese. She just told me she's Irish. Isn't that illegal?

MISS SCOTT: It's not illegal. It's…just not encouraged.

RICHARD: I think it should be illegal.

YVETTE: Nobody cares what you think, you idiot!

MISS SCOTT: Yvette! In the corner. Now!

YVETTE: The other students "ooooooh." Miss Scott silences them with a snap of her fingers. I find a corner and stand in it.

MISS SCOTT: You will stand there, silently, until recess. Hopefully that'll teach you to behave like a proper young lady and not some feral child.

        Pause.

YVETTE: I hate grade six.

Scene 6

YVETTE: Dr. Thompson came back to visit us later in the week.

DR. THOMPSON: Rheumatic fever. If I'd known earlier I could've treated it sooner. The worst is over. But you might feel some exhaustion and shortness of breath. You need to rest as much as you can. Do not stress your body. I'm going to tell Yvette to watch you.

KATHERINE: My jailer. She's always watching me.

YVETTE: Dr. Thompson, I want to be a doctor but Miss Scott says I can't.

DR. THOMPSON: Of course you can be a doctor—if you study hard enough. The world is changing faster and faster. If the Russkies can shoot sputnik into orbit then you can be a doctor. Tell Miss Scott I said so.

YVETTE: As much as I wanted to tell Miss Scott "Dr. Thompson said I can be a doctor. So there!" I didn't. But I just think it really hard whenever I see her.

                YVETTE makes a face, showing how hard she's concentrating.

                Pageant day! The parents were packed into our tiny school gym. Everyone was forgetting their lines. Miss Scott kept snapping her fingers and whispering lines whenever someone froze. I was the only one who didn't need any whispers. When we were finished, all of the parents clapped and cheered. I got to take a bow. On stage. With all of the other students.

                We're walking home after the play. It is early evening. A slight chill in the air. My mama hobbles along as fast as she can.

                Miss Scott says I'm the best Indian she ever saw.

                Mama laughs when I say that.

                Mama tucks me in and I dream about being on stage and the audience cheering for me after the play.

CHARLIE: Yvette! Your breakfast is getting cold!

YVETTE: I'm coming I'm coming! Geeeze, it's not even eight yet. (*Calling.*) Mama, breakfast!

                No answer.

Mama! Get up. It's time for breakfast.

Pause.

Mom?

She lies down on the bed.

I put my arms around her. She got colder and colder and colder.

Pause.

The graveyard in Allistair isn't big. Some old headstones. Lots of weeds. The sun is shining. We can't afford a headstone so mama only gets a wooden cross.

"Katherine Wong 1921-1957" is painted on it. No one from the reserve came to the funeral. Many Chinese men are comforting my father. The only white people are Reverend Smith, his wife and Dr. Thompson. Once Reverend Smith is done with the final prayer, they're gone. At the café, my dad serves tea to the men. No one speaks English. Once they're gone, it's just me and Dad. He stares at the floor.

(To CHARLIE.) Dad?

CHARLIE: I don't know how much longer we can stay here.

YVETTE: Papa?

CHARLIE: We have to move.

YVETTE: Yes, Papa.

CHARLIE: It's just you and me now.

Pause. Blackout.

End of Act I.

Act II

Scene 1

A school desk, a bed, a mirror, a kitchen table, pizza boxes, a periodic table. Saskatoon, Saskatchewan, 1963. YVETTE enters, piecing together the images from her memory. She's 16.

YVETTE: After Mama died, Dad and I moved to Saskatoon. *(She picks up a pizza box.)* Dad works in a pizza restaurant now. We get a lot of leftover pizza for supper. I think I'm getting fat. *(She turns her butt to the mirror.)* These jeans are making my bum look big.

She opens her school bag and spills out her books onto the kitchen table and starts doing homework. CHARLIE enters. He's a little drunk.

CHARLIE: Ah, you're home. I didn't hear you come in. What are you doing there? *(He looks at her books.)* What is this? All these numbers? *(Sounding out the title.)* Cal-cu...cal-cuh...

YVETTE: Calculus. It's a type of math.

CHARLIE: A "type" of math? How many different types are there? Isn't one enough? And what do you need to learn it for?

YVETTE: Did your shift end early? I didn't expect you here.

CHARLIE: Business is a little slow. Boss said I could take a couple of days off.

YVETTE: Business isn't slow. He's been drinking again. Dad is the best cook they've got. The boss looks the other way when Dad's had too many. The apartment gets really small when he's like this. He hovers. Goes through my books, examining them, shaking his head.

CHARLIE: More than one type of math. Unnecessary.

YVETTE: He usually goes to his room and sleeps it off. But he's still here. Slumping in his chair. Staring at the apartment.

(To CHARLIE.) What is it, Dad?

CHARLIE sighs heavily.

CHARLIE: I should go back to China. Hong Kong. We should move. There's nothing for us here.

YVETTE: Hong Kong! Dad, what are you talking about?

CHARLIE: I can take care of you better there. Find you a husband.

YVETTE: I'm only 16.

CHARLIE: And I'm old! China will be better. For us.

YVETTE: I'm trying not to panic. *(To CHARLIE.)* Dad, get some sleep.

He nods and shuffles to his room. Leaning on the wall for support. I hope it's because he's drunk. But he's also looks really old. China! I can't go to China!

A school bell rings.

YVETTE: I like school. It gets me out of our apartment. But I'm graduating this year. I wish I could go to school forever. Mr. Tanner is my favourite teacher. Math and physics. He doesn't think calculus is unnecessary.

MR. TANNER: OK class, please pick up your papers before you run off for dinner. Miss Wong, could you please stay for a minute. You got 100 percent on your assignment. And you did all the extra questions and got them right as well. I can only give you 100 percent.

YVETTE: They were fun to do.

MR. TANNER: *(Laughs.)* They were fun? They're not meant to be fun, they're meant to be challenging.

YVETTE: That's why they're fun.

MR. TANNER: I wish the other students thought so. Have you given any thought towards university? Your marks are phenomenal—top of the class.

YVETTE: University? I have to talk to my dad about that. See if we can afford it.

MR. TANNER: Afford it? You won't have to worry about "affording it." Not with your grades. Apply for a scholarship, Yvette. There's plenty of money out there. You want me to look into that for you?

YVETTE: Sure, thank you.

MR. TANNER: But I also have some good news. You're the class valedictorian. Congratulations.

YVETTE: I'm the what?

MR. TANNER: You were a shoe-in. No one has come close to the grades you have. You'll be the first Chinese student to give the valedictory address. You're making history, Yvette. I'm sure it won't be the last time.

YVETTE: I have to make a speech? In front of everyone? But he ignores me.

MR. TANNER: Is there anything else, Yvette?

YVETTE: It's just…family stuff.

MR. TANNER: Maybe you should talk to one of your friends.

YVETTE: Friends? Oh sure. I got lots of them.

School bell rings. She picks up a tray.

God, the cafeteria is serving pizza for dinner! I just had pizza for breakfast and I'm pretty sure I'll be having it for supper too. I hate pizza! *(She spots MAGGIE.)*

Who's that?

An Indian girl sits by herself at one of the tables.

I've never seen her before. Must be new. No one goes near her. She doesn't seem to care. She keeps sipping her coke and flipping the pages of a fashion magazine. *Vogue*, I think. *(YVETTE stares.)*

Uh-oh. She's looking right at me—caught me staring.

She smiles. I try to smile back. *(Smiles uncomfortably.)*

"Gook!" Gook? She points at me and yells it again, louder, "GOOK!" The others look at who she's pointing at and they all stare at me. Some of them laugh, "Gook, that's a good one."

(She drops the tray.) I run away.

(Pause.) The library is much safer anyway. Almost no one goes in there. Gook? No one's ever called me that before. I hope I don't see that girl again.

Scene 2

YVETTE sits at the library, staring at her books.

YVETTE: I hate Fridays. The library stays open till five and they let me stay. I don't want to go home.

MAGGIE: So what you in for?

YVETTE: God! She scared me. It's the Indian girl. She sits next to me spilling a bunch of fashion mags on the table. She smiles again.

MAGGIE: What's this? *(Grabs one of YVETTE's books.)* Calculus 200? Are these university books? God, the crap we got is hard enough. Is this part of detention for you?

YVETTE: I'm studying.

MAGGIE: Studying! It's Friday. After school. I mean, really? Me, I'm burning off some DT hours. Studying for what? I thought you Chinks were all super smart and didn't need to study or nothing.

YVETTE: I'm not... What? Super smart? A Chink? *(To MAGGIE.)* Don't call me a Chink. Please. Or a gook.

MAGGIE: Sorry. I thought you were Chinese.

YVETTE: I am…but…how would you like it if I pointed at you and screamed "Squaaaaaw" at the top of lungs and then did this?

              YVETTE quietly war whoops.

MAGGIE: Your technique is all wrong. It's more like this.

              MAGGIE war whoops loudly.

YVETTE: Shhhhhhh. We're in a library.

MAGGIE: Well, if you're going to whoop then you whoop like you mean it. My name's Maggie.

YVETTE: Yvette.

MAGGIE: Pleased to meet you. I just moved here. Like last week or something. I can't wait to get out of here, myself. You have a boyfriend yet? I think my height scares the boys. They're all afraid of the half-breed girl who's taller than them.

She laughs. Pause.

YVETTE: What's a half-breed?

MAGGIE: *(Laughing.)* You're kidding me, right? Half Breed? Half Indian, half white. My dad's white. An Englishman, actually. My mom's Indian. From a reserve in Nova Scotia. She's a Micmac. He was in the Royal Navy and they met in Halifax. Troooo love. You've got to be some kind of half breed too, I think. You're not all Chinaman are you?

YVETTE: Is she ever going to shut up?

MAGGIE: So do you do this a lot? Hide out in the library with your nose buried in a book no one told you to read?

YVETTE: I don't know. I just never thought about it.

MAGGIE: What are you doing after this?

YVETTE: I was going to go home and… *(Pause.)* study.

MAGGIE: Study some more! Wow. You're one craaaayzeee Chinaman. Come on, it's Friday. Show me what kind of fun you can have in Saskatoon. I'm sure someone's throwing a party somewhere.

YVETTE: I haven't been invited to any.

MAGGIE: What are you? In kindergarten or something? You don't need an invitation. You just find out where the party's happening and show up.

YVETTE: I can't…just go to a stranger's house.

MAGGIE: Stranger? How long have you been going to this school?

YVETTE: Four years.

MAGGIE: Oh god, I knew you weren't the most popular kid here but I didn't know you were "that kid." *(She sighs and shakes her head.)* So when do I pick you up?

YVETTE: Pardon me?

MAGGIE: Look, you want to be "that kid" for the rest of your life? Of course not. And I just can't show up at a party alone. Understand?

YVETTE: No, I don't understand.

MAGGIE: Indian girl, by herself, with these "good white chillens." Are you kidding me?

YVETTE: I thought you were only half-Indian.

MAGGIE: Did you think I was only "half-Indian" when you first saw me? Look, Chinese girls are "exotic." Interesting but not threatening. Plus, you're the school genius. They'll have no choice but to let me in if I show up with you. You could make a friend or two. *(Pause.)* Come on. It'll be fun.

YVETTE: OK. I'll meet you at the…the…the what? Where do people meet to be picked up? She waits. Then she smiles.

MAGGIE: You really are a special case. Meet me at the corner store. Nine o'clock.

YVETTE: Isn't that kind of late? But she walks away laughing. A party! What am I thinking? *(At home.)* Dad's not home. We haven't seen much of each other since he said he's moving us to Hong Kong. Which is fine by me. I'm trying avoid him as much as possible.

> *She opens some books and tries to read. She's alone. It weighs on her. She stares at her books.*

Damnit! OK Maggie. I'll go to your stupid party. She's waiting for me at the corner store.

MAGGIE: You're wearing that? Those are your school clothes.

YVETTE: It's not like anyone's going to notice what I'm wearing.

MAGGIE: Trust me, everyone will notice. You're going out. You're going to have fun. You want people to notice that, not that you're in your school duds. We're not getting into any parties like this. Come on. Let's fix you up.

YVETTE: Fix me up, how?

MAGGIE: Hey. One night is all I'm asking. Alright? On Monday, you can go back to being "that kid." Tonight though, nah-ah. You're going to be an Yvette they won't forget. Hey, that rhymes!

YVETTE: Yeah, clever.

MAGGIE: We're going to my place. I might have some clothes that'll fit ya.

YVETTE: She doesn't wait for an answer. She grabs my hand and drags me to her house.

> *A flurry of skirts, blouses, scarves, boots and shoes and YVETTE is transformed. She looks at herself in the mirror. The clothes are a little big, but with a tuck and pull here and there, they fit.*

MAGGIE: OK. Now your face.

YVETTE: What's wrong with my face?

MAGGIE: Nothing. You're just not showing it off. Hold still.

> *YVETTE is made up.*

Not bad, not bad. Didn't your mom teach you this stuff?

YVETTE: She died when I was ten.

MAGGIE: Aaah, really? Sorry. *(Finishes up.)* There. No one will recognize you now.

           YVETTE ponders herself in the mirror.

YVETTE: She's right. Even I don't recognize myself.

           She wobbles in the boots. MAGGIE laughs.

MAGGIE: Don't worry. We're not walking far.

           MAGGIE pulls out a mickey and offers it to YVETTE.

           This'll steady your gait.

YVETTE: No thanks.

MAGGIE: Suit yourself.

           MAGGIE cracks the seal and takes a shot.

           I don't suppose you smoke either?

           Offers YVETTE a smoke. She shakes her head.

           Gauloises. French.

           She lights it and inhales deeply.

           Like Anna Karina, *n'est-ce pas*?

YVETTE: Who?

MAGGIE: Oh lord, I am in the hinterland, aren't I? Anna Karina. She's a movie star. Married to Jean-Luc Godard. He's a very famous French director.

YVETTE: She laughs again and grabs a *Vogue* magazine from a pile next to her bed.

MAGGIE: *(Tapping a page.)* There. That's Anna Karina. She's beautiful. The way she purses her lips, tilts her head. French women just know how to seduce a camera. Once I'm done school, I'm going to go to Paris and become a model.

YVETTE: She grabs my hand and drags me out of the house. *(To MAGGIE.)* Do you know where you're going?

MAGGIE: It's not like we're going to get lost. This ain't a big city. Hong Kong, now that's a city you can get lost in. Easily. London too.

YVETTE: You lived in Hong Kong?

MAGGIE: Yeah. Before dad moved us here we lived all over the world. Mostly in England. But also Hong Kong, Bermuda, Cyprus, Egypt—

YVETTE: Egypt! You've been to Egypt? Did you see the pyramids?

MAGGIE: *(Laughing.)* Yeah, I've seen the pyramids. Rode a camel. Didn't see any mummies though.

YVETTE: What are they like? The pyramids, I mean. I've wanted to see the pyramids since I was a little girl.

MAGGIE: Big. Stony. Dusty. Don't know what else to tell you. I was only seven so I didn't see what the big deal was. I preferred the Red Sea. The beaches are beautiful and you could go swimming in it. I did some snorkeling and saw a shark. Swam right underneath me. That was pretty groovy.

YVETTE: Groovy? That's all you can say is that it's "groovy?" I mean, how many people get to see a shark or the pyramids or ride a camel before they're out of high school and that's the best you can say is that it's groovy. *(Pause.)* She stares at me. I can tell she's trying not to laugh.

MAGGIE: Hey. I'm going to need you to be a little less cranky if we're going to pull this off.

     Pause.

YVETTE: Can I have a cigarette?

MAGGIE considers.

MAGGIE: Sure. But maybe you'll want a drop of this first. Just to relax you a little.

YVETTE: She offers the bottle again. This time I take it. I sniff it. It burns my nostrils.

MAGGIE: What are you, a connoisseur or something?

YVETTE: I take a small sip. Yeeugh! (*She makes a face.*) But I take another sip. More this time.

MAGGIE: Easy there. We need to save some for the party.

YVETTE: She takes the bottle then hands me a cigarette. I take it.

She stares at it.

MAGGIE: It's not a bug! Put it in your mouth.

She puts in her mouth. MAGGIE lights a match.

Lean in. It ain't gonna light itself. Quickly. Ow!

She drops the match and waves her hand to cool it.

A little quicker next time.

She lights another match. YVETTE tilts her head and dips the cigarette into the flame.

You have to inhale or it won't catch.

YVETTE inhales quickly then doubles over in a coughing spasm.

(*Laughing.*) OK, champ. We'll stick to this for now. (*Shows the mickey.*) Let's go find some fun.

YVETTE: We meander around the neighbourhood. I tell her we're lost. She says we're fine.

Early 1960s rock music in the distance.

MAGGIE: See. I told you we'd find it.

YVETTE: I freeze. Here we are. In front of a big house. *(To MAGGIE.)* I'm not sure about this— She links her arm in mine and marches us to the front door and strolls in like she owns the place.

The music suddenly stops. A spot on YVETTE.

I'm waiting to be told I don't belong here. I'm waiting for someone to throw us out. I'm waiting for them to laugh at us. I'm waiting for them to scream "Gook!" I'm waiting for the worst moment of my life.

Music returns.

MAGGIE: Hey, I'm Maggie. This is Yvette. You guys know Yvette, right? Of course you do. Yeah, I didn't recognize her either. If you ever need help at math, this is the girl you want to see. *(Pops a cigarette into her mouth.)* Oh these? Gauloises. Believe me, they're impossible to find in Saskatoon. I had to sneak these in the last time I was in Paris. You have! I just adore that city.

YVETTE: I can't believe it. We're surrounded by all these girls. They hang off her every word. She's sexy. Sophisticated. Someone hands us punch. Maggie boldly pulls the mickey out. The girls gasp. She pours a good dollop into her own glass. No effort to hide it at all. That's it, I think. These are "good kids." They won't tolerate this! She winks at me and smiles then pours a little into my glass. The gasps have turned to "oooohs." I'm no longer invisible. I am now "noticed." Maggie's firm grip on my arm keeps me upright. She holds the mickey out, silently inviting the other girls to join in. Nervous hands thrust out, wanting to be a world-travelling French movie star as well.

YVETTE slams back the punch. the music fades.

Pause. She rushes off stage and hurls, loudly, over and over again. CHARLIE enters.

CHARLIE: Yvette? Yvette? You sick? *(Pounds on the door.)* What's wrong? You sick? Yvette?

YVETTE opens the door. Her make-up is a mess.

What's wrong with your face? And these clothes? Where'd you get these clothes?

He leans in and smells YVETTE's breath.

Ahhhh. You're that kind of sick. We got a letter from someone. *(He hands her the envelope.)* It looks important. Is it from the government?

YVETTE: It's from the university.

CHARLIE: University? Why would the university be writing to you?

YVETTE opens the envelope.

YVETTE: I've been accepted with a scholarship. Wow, Mr. Tanner works fast.

CHARLIE: We can't afford university!

YVETTE: It's with a scholarship. It means they'll pay for my tuition and books.

CHARLIE: Will they also pay for food? A place to live? Clothes?

YVETTE: No, dad, but…

CHARLIE: We have no family here.

YVETTE: We have no family in China, either. You said they all died in the war.

CHARLIE: I've made arrangements. We won't have to live like this much longer.

YVETTE: If I become a doctor then I can take care of us.

CHARLIE: When? When will you become a doctor?

YVETTE: Eight years. Ten. I don't know.

            He doesn't answer me and goes to his room. He leans against the wall to help himself down the hallway. He hasn't been drinking today. *(Pause.)* Ten years might be too long.

            She changes out of MAGGIE's clothes and puts them in a paper bag.

Scene 3

School bell.

MR. TANNER: Ahhh, Yvette. Could I see you for a minute?

YVETTE: Mr. Tanner?

MR. TANNER: Some of the other students told me that you were seen hanging around with Maggie Wolfe this weekend. Look, you probably don't have a lot of experience with Indians. Just stay away from them. They're trouble.

YVETTE: Trouble, Mr. Tanner?

MR. TANNER: I heard she brought alcohol to a party. Was that true?

YVETTE: Well, yes but—

MR. TANNER: She did?

YVETTE: A lump forms in my throat. I think I just got Maggie into trouble. Serious trouble. *(To MR. TANNER.)* But…but…the other kids were drinking as well. Oh geeze, really? Is that going to make things better?

MR. TANNER: Yvette, these are good kids. You're a good kid. You all have your futures to think about. None of you need a corrupting influence like Maggie messing that up for you. You understand me? Indians are trouble. Just stay away from them.

YVETTE: *(Whispering.)* I have a secret. I promise not to tell.

MR. TANNER: Now. You should be getting some forms from the University of Saskatchewan. Just get your dad to sign them and you're all set.

YVETTE: Why does he need to sign them?

MR. TANNER: Because you're a minor.

> *YVETTE fights tears.*

What's wrong, Yvette?

YVETTE: What if he won't sign them?

MR. TANNER: What do you mean, "won't sign them?" It's an amazing scholarship. Any father would be proud to sign them.

YVETTE: He won't sign them, Mr. Tanner.

> *Pause.*

MR. TANNER: This is your future, Yvette.

YVETTE: That's it? That's all the advice he's going to give me?

MR. TANNER: And remember what I said about Maggie. Nothing but trouble. Stay away from her.

YVETTE: OK. Thanks.

The rest of the day is a blur. I don't see Maggie until near the end of school.

> *Holds out the bag.*

Hey, thanks for the clothes. I had fun. At least I think I did.

MAGGIE: Don't talk to me you rat! I don't ever want to see you again.

YVETTE: What?

MAGGIE: I got suspended because someone told Mr. Tanner that I brought booze to the party. I wasn't the only one, you know. Or don't you remember?

YVETTE: Look, I'm sorry—

MAGGIE: Shut up. You got your life all figure out. It's all so easy for you. But you just messed up my plans to go to Paris. My parents are gonna kill me when they find out about this.

MAGGIE grabs the bag and throws it onto the floor.

And keep these stupid clothes. I don't ever want to see them or you again.

YVETTE: Maggie…

But she stormed away. Suspended? And just when I think this day can't get any worse I see Aunt Doris by our apartment.

DORIS: Little girl! Oh my god, you're not so little anymore.

YVETTE: I wish people would stop saying that!

DORIS: How are you?

YVETTE: What are you doing here?

Oh god, that sounds so much like my mom. It's too late to take it back.

DORIS: I'm wondering how you're doing. We haven't seen

you in a long time. We didn't know what happened after you left Allistair…after your mama died. We only found out after I tried to visit you guys. *(Tries not to cry.)* How come no one told us?

YVETTE: I'm not supposed to talk to you. Please don't come here anymore.

DORIS: Why are you saying that?

YVETTE: I rush inside and lock the door. I hope no one saw her here. I've got enough to worry about without her showing up.

> *DORIS knocks on the door.*

She pleads for me to open the door. I pretend I don't hear.

DORIS: *(Weeping.)* Little girl, please, Yvette. Please. I just want to talk to you. To see you again.

YVETTE: I wish she'd just go away. I try to read but I can still hear her outside. I hide in the bathroom. Really! I'm hiding in my own bathroom. I can't believe I'm doing this. Why am I doing this? What am I so afraid of? *(She realizes just how lonely she is.)* Oh god, I wish so much my mom was here.

Scene 4

> *CHARLIE enters. He moves slowly. Hobbling to his chair. He brings a pizza and puts it on the table. He pulls out a mickey, uncaps it, and pours some into a glass. He drinks some then reaches for a piece of pizza. He looks at YVETTE's books that are still on the table and shakes his head. YVETTE enters and approaches.*

CHARLIE: New kind of pizza. Ham and pineapple. Boss calls it "Hawaiian." Pineapple. On a pizza. Such silliness.

(Takes a bite.) Hmmmm. Not bad. Have some. *(She doesn't want any.)* You're not eating. What's wrong? You sick?

YVETTE: Daddy, I really want to go to university.

CHARLIE: It's not your decision.

YVETTE: Will I be able to go to university there?

CHARLIE: I will find you a husband. Someone who can take care of the both of us. At least we'll be around our own people.

YVETTE: You mean your people. I'm not Chinese.

CHARLIE: You are Chinese!

YVETTE: Not like you. I don't speak or read the language. You never taught it to me.

CHARLIE: I tried teaching it to you but your mother made me stop. She said she didn't want you to sound funny when you talk. "You're not Chinese." You think you're a white woman? Like your mother pretended to be? Ha! Well, you're a smart girl, you'll pick it up.

YVETTE: He leaves to his room. God, why couldn't my life be a math problem!

> *She picks up the forms and is about to rip them. She smooths them out, looks down the hallway, then signs them and puts them in her books. She picks up her books.*

I feel sick. I keep thinking the forms will fall out and get blown away by the wind. I want them to fall out. Oh god, what am I doing? I can't do this. I'm going to go to jail.

DORIS: Little girl!

YVETTE: I jump out of my skin. *(To DORIS.)* Auntie Doris!

You can't be here! People will see. Go away, please. Just go away.

School bell rings in the distance.

YVETTE: I gotta go. I don't want to be late for school. I hope no one saw us. But she won't let up.

DORIS: Yvette, please, I just want to talk to you. Just for a second. OK. Just one second. You can give me that, at least.

YVETTE: OK, OK, just a second. Please make it quick.

DORIS: You look so much like your mother. And that makes it harder to see you, knowing that she's gone. We were so close and then…then nothing…just silence and anger. If she knew she was dying I know she wouldn't want it to end that way—with us not talking. You're the only connection I have to her anymore. I miss her so much, Yvette. I can't tell you how much I miss her.

YVETTE: I miss her too.

            And then I see it. She looks exactly like my mom. I miss my mom so much I just give her a great big hug. I don't want her to talk, I don't want to say anything that'll break the spell. I just want to hold my mom. She holds me and whispers calming "shhhhh-shhhhhhh-shhhhh" and rocks me gently.

She rocks in place as she is hugged. Pause.

DORIS: You've grown so big, I have to reach up to kiss you.

YVETTE: The spell is broken. *(To DORIS.)* How did you find me?

DORIS: I looked for you. And I wasn't going to stop until I found you.

YVETTE: Mr. Tanner suddenly interrupts.

MR. TANNER: Is everything alright, Yvette? Is this woman bothering you?

DORIS: I'm her aunt. I'm not bothering her!

MR. TANNER: On her father's side?

DORIS: I'm her mother's sister! Who are you?

YVETTE: It's alright, Auntie Doris. He's my teacher. *(To MR. TANNER.)* Mr. Tanner, this is Doris, my aunt.

"I see… Don't be late for class."

And he walks back towards the school.

(To DORIS.) Mom said never to tell anyone I was Indian. He thinks I'm only Chinese. He told me Indians are trouble.

DORIS: Well, he'd be right if he met your mom and had that attitude.

YVETTE: I have to go. Class is starting soon.

DORIS: I want to see you again.

YVETTE: Sure. You know where we live. Dad's usually home after eight.

She gives me another hug. Mr. Tanner's class is first. I take my desk and wait. But Mr. Tanner waves me over.

MR. TANNER: Did you have a chance to talk to your dad about the scholarship?

YVETTE: I don't say anything. I just hand him the forms. With my dad's forged signature. He holds them for a minute, looking them over. Then he rips them in half.

MR. TANNER: I misjudged you, Yvette. I can't, in good conscience, have my name attached to your application.

YVETTE: Is this about my dad—

MR. TANNER: It's about you, Yvette. You and Maggie bringing alcohol to a party? You jeopardized the future of a lot of innocent kids. I tried to have you suspended but the principal wouldn't hear of it. Because of your grades. But he did agree that you should not be the class valedictorian. That wouldn't be the correct example we want to set for the other students.

YVETTE: And then he dismisses me with a wave. I'm not one of the "good kids" anymore. Now that he knows my secret. I leave the classroom. I ignore the bell and leave the school. I've never done this but it's now colder. Hostile. I don't want to be here anymore. *(She screams.)* Auuuuuuugh!

> *She paces, frustrated. Then stops.*

Maggie! *(Knocks on the door.)* Please, please, please let me in. *(Knocks again, louder.)* Maggie! It's me, Yvette! Please let me in. I just want to talk to you. Please! *(Pause, no answer.)* I'm sorry, OK. I'm so sorry. I didn't want you to get suspended. I just… Mr. Tanner…I can't lie to him. I know it's not fair but…I'm just sorry, OK. I'm so sorry. *(Pause.)* Maggie?

She doesn't answer. I'm sure she's in there. She was the closest I came to having a friend and I screwed it up. I hate my life. My dad was right, there is nothing for us here.

> *She throws her books away and mopes. She sits at the table with a pen and notepad. CHARLIE enters.*

CHARLIE: What are you doing? More homework?

YVETTE: I'm writing a letter.

CHARLIE: A letter to who?

YVETTE: To Mom.

CHARLIE: Why do you want to do that?

YVETTE: Because I miss her.

Dad sits next to me.

CHARLIE: Me too. I miss her too. Tell her I tried my best. Will you say that for me in your letter?

YVETTE: Of course, Daddy. *(Pause.)* I saw Doris today.

CHARLIE: Doris? Today? When today?

YVETTE: Outside of school. I told her she could come visit anytime. I hope that's alright.

CHARLIE: Yes, yes, of course. Doris. It's been years. I better make sure I have tea. She loves her tea. Did she say anything about Amos? I wonder how he's doing.

Scene 5

School bell. YVETTE with her books.

YVETTE: I got reprimanded for skipping. Mr. Tanner doesn't chat with me after class. The extra questions aren't fun anymore. Maggie hasn't come back. I can't wait for school to end. I don't want to go to my graduation ceremony but Auntie Doris says I have to.

DORIS: You're the first in our family to graduate, of course you're going!

YVETTE: She's bossy…like my mom. She now lives in Saskatoon and works as a waitress. She visits us almost every week. She and Dad sit in the back of the auditorium when I get my diploma. *(Pause.)* I barely hear the speech from the valedictorian about how the "future is ours to grasp." My future is in

Hong Kong—and some unknown husband who will take care of my old father. Maybe he will let me go to university there. *(Pause.)* Dad and I start packing. He writes on the boxes…in Chinese. It makes him happy. He seems less old. He barely drinks. Maggie said, Hong Kong is a city you can get lost in. I feel lost already and I'm still in Saskatoon. Since school is over, I have nothing to do in the day. *(She finds her book about ancient Egypt. She looks through it.)* It's not the same in books.

CHARLIE: You don't need to pack all your books. You won't need them now. Unnecessary.

              Pause.

YVETTE: I'm not going.

CHARLIE: It's not your decision!

YVETTE: It's my future. If you have to go to Hong Kong, then you go. I'm staying and I'm going to university.

CHARLIE: Who will take care of you?

YVETTE: I don't know! You? Auntie Doris? It doesn't matter. I'll figure it out. *(Pause.)* He looks away. He knows I'm not bluffing. His shoulders heave like Mushom Amos's did when I waved good-bye to him. He leaves the apartment. Staggering. Seeking comfort in a bottle.

              I'm sorry, Daddy. I'm sorry…

Scene 6

              YVETTE is now an adult. She puts the pizza boxes, bed, table, mirror and desk away. She picks up the letter.

YVETTE: Dear Mama. I miss you. Today, more than ever. You were right about our secret. I didn't tell anyone. I

never did. But my favourite teacher, Mr. Tanner, found out this morning and he ripped up my dreams of going to university, of being a doctor, of taking care of dad. Just because I am an Indian. I need you, right now, more than ever. I don't know what to do and I'm afraid. All my love, Yvette. *(Puts away the letter, looks around, holds her grad gown.)* Mama, today I am a doctor because you told me I could if I really wanted to. The university still gave me the scholarship. They didn't care what Mr. Tanner thought. I am graduating at the top of my class. My dreams didn't die. So what am I afraid of now, Mama? *(Pause.)* I have to give a speech to my classmates and I don't know what to say.

DORIS: Little girl. We're all so proud of you. *(Hands her a small leather folder.)* Mushom wants you to have this. We know what your mama said…about being an Indian…but we want you to know how much we love you. No matter what.

YVETTE opens the folder. It reveals an eagle feather.

YVETTE: Thank you, Auntie.

Mama, I'm no longer afraid. I need to tell them my mother was a Cree Indian…and that I am proud to be your daughter.

She puts on the gown, holds up the feather. She turns to face her classmates.

I have a story to tell you, about when I first dreamed of being a doctor.

Pause. Blackout.

The End.